DEAD WHITE MEN

SHANE

RHODES

COACH HOUSE BOOKS, TORONTO

Canada Council **Conseil des Arts**
for the Arts du Canada

 ONTARIO ARTS COUNCIL
CONSEIL DES ARTS DE L'ONTARIO
an Ontario government agency
un organisme du gouvernement de l'Ontario

Canadä

Published with the generous assistance of the Canada Council for the Arts
and the Ontario Arts Council. Coach House Books also acknowledges the
support of the Government of Canada through the Canada Book Fund and
the Government of Ontario through the Ontario Book Publishing Tax Credit.

LIBRARY AND ARCHIVES CANADA CATALOGUING IN PUBLICATION

Rhodes, Shane, 1973-, author
    Dead white men / Shane Rhodes.

Poems.
Issued in print and electronic formats.
ISBN 978-1-55245-345-2

    I. Title.

PS8585.H568D43 2017   C811'.6   C2017-900542-1

Dead White Men is available as an ebook: ISBN 978 1 77056 345 2

Purchase of the print version of this book entitles you to a free digital copy.
To claim your ebook of this title, please email sales@chbooks.com with
proof of purchase. (Coach House Books reserves the right to terminate the
free digital download offer at any time.)

for Katherine

Dead White Men

Men
with all their acumen and little melanin.
            Men with their pens and manuscripts and little pots of ink.
        Men with their sails and ships, those little pots of stink.
      Brilliant men (all eminent andrologicians), let them
                manipulate you in their immanence,
            diminish you in their abandonment.

See the glow of their monocled manvision,
            their helicopters rhythmically slapping the wind?
      We shall raze monuments to them and lament
their chimeric commandments.
                  Men sans pigment searching the firmament
            for fragments of land, something immense
in the mangrove to smear their names upon,

            something to dominate with their unsheathed instruments.
      Unabashed men maniform in their manners
      (AKA manacles of manwhim), emancipated
            in the sheaves of their manicured fascicles.
            Appalling men, the shear sheen of their mandates.

See men meeting other men, hands raised?

 This, gentlemen, captured in the woodcut

at the map's edge, is pinnacle of their movement.

From sea to sea, men annulling.

 Men kindly given to husbandry and savagery,

 to balladry and bastardry, to many things sundry

and the bawdy Vice of Buggery, but never to drudgery

 (all that shelter!) or laundry (all those sheets!).

 Men, their quadrants fixed to the horizon,

eye the menses of the moon.

 Of course the Englishmen menaced Frenchmen

 who contradicted the Germans for complimenting Scotsmen

whimpering to Tasmans for mangling their Yeomen

 who demanded more Seamen from their Laymen.

 When the men write 'her,'

 they are often referring to their ships.

 When, demented for hymen, the men write

 'I put her politeness to every test,'

they may not be referring to their ships.

7

An argument in the armament,
a battle in the battlement,
a testicle in the testament:
we must manage our men.

As the protest goes by (hear the common lament), men
man the margins shaking their batons –
in the poem, I raise my cellphone
into the wind to record this moment
and the lustre of its enforcement.
See their dead white faces in the crumpling map-scrolls of surf?
This is men, dormant in their element.

Look at them examining the mental movements
of other men, the requirements of their virilesence,
the sentiments of their women, the regulation of their enjoyments –
they jot their masculine medicaments
and mansplain in perfect diction
that they have done this for us,
for all of us: meaning us men.

Bemantled with medals from their queens,
rattling with ornaments from their kings,

men slash their names into the mute trees: the forests for men.

These, our forefathers, men who would judge:

Not man enough! Not white enough! Not dead enough!

I am but a simple man, dickered with doubt,

tanned pinkish beige by my computer screen,

uncovering documents of men discovering men –

manipulative amanuensis to their dictation,

I shell poems from prose and give them home.

Immense in their engagements, manifold

in their entanglements, the cannons rage a common hymn

of the establishments: all white, all men.

This: an amended amen to the ornamental sacrament

within the parliament of men.

what is history

a whitish story

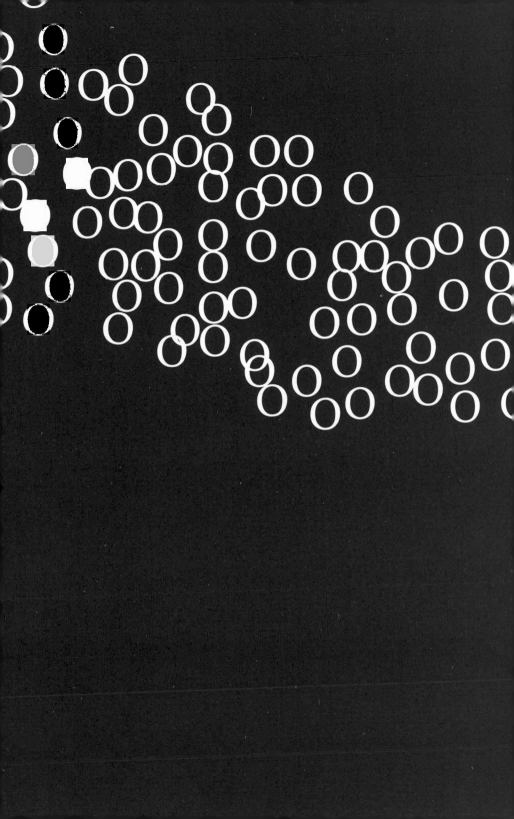

All Well
after John Franklin

1.

At six, I managed a measurement
and the Temp was fifty. We halted,
rested, observed the question: our companions,
their bodies smelling like carrion.
We continued our progress then encamped,
sore feet, weary. Lat 66 53 50. A herd
of twenty Musk Ox (exactly), exchanged misgivings
on the Halifax Livre and I read the compass course
– ten degrees off true north. Groundcover of footprints,
yet of men I record with shaking pen
on a page rubbed raw against my chest,
I am the first. We remained all evening
with heavy thirst. I put my hand to his breast
and drew the halfbreed close: rank and rankless.
My bowels hurt. Such weathers,
your most high and caesarean Prince,
move through me at times with load-bearing violence,
yet how your stars light a corpse!

2.

I was opposed by a gale north northwest
driving us far without a southing.
It's the worst and I want
to rage against it
as I rage against
any failure I have no hope to resist.
Gazing now at this disorient
moment, I've put it all at risk.
We supped on carrion bones and the acrid nerve cord left
by wolves. The cold white
against our famished bodies like the chest
of a living animal split
open – the organs quivering wet
with spittle.
Is this the passivity
I was promised?
To the monolith, Master,
a dangling magnetized needle,
we suffer shoes half eaten.
But, Cape Turnagain,
that point,
I named it.

3.

We could see no opening.
At nine p.m. brilliant coruscations of the Aurora Borealis appeared, an arched form
of a pale ochre colour with a slight tinge of red.
The compass quivered.
Is there another world elsewhere
more than this patterned mess?
It crossed my mind
to the NW.
and I concluded that man
is an animal
impelled in circles –
this tack, now that,
in a state of ceaseless motion.
For the record, the wind was favourable until the eighth.
By the side of the unnamed lake,
we fired cannons
to notify the savages
and savaged them.
With their brown hands, they rubbed my continence red.
Ever Your Faithful Servant,
I tire not, Dear Lord,
for public good
or to acquire.

The Tragicall End of Henry Hudson
after Abacuk Pricket

1.

All could see our course as the Ice
did lye.

§

Hearing the rut of sea ashoare,
wee weighed, stood, then let flye
towards the north.

thwart the Iles of *Faro*

Wee fell into a fogge.

raysed the Iles of *Westmonie*

Saw *Mount Hecla* cast out her fire
and were embayed.

Groneland proved a foggie banke

§

Some men fell sicke.
I will not say it was for feare.

though God only knew what we were doing here

2.

Unto the snowy Rockes
wee haled aground our broody ship

and in the snow I saw the footing of a man.

                                                            as if enplinthed

                                    §

After three moneths in a Labyrinth
of Ice, this was November first.

By the tenth, we were frozen in.

                                    §

To speake of all our Winter troubles
would bee tedious.

                                    §

His nails froze off.

                                            it was hideous

3.

In our hunger, wee spurned not the mosse
                        (the powder of a post would bee much better)
nor the Frogge
                                    (as loathsome as a Toade)
nor the Cockle-grasse.

                                    §

Then came a Savage with a Sled.

Being our first, our M^r gave him
a Knife, Buttons,
and a Looking-glasse.

Upon two beaver skinnes,
the Savage laid the Knife and Glass
and the Buttons upon a Morse's Teeth.

(which, I have learned, is a type of horse
with a Seal beneath)

§

In our extremitie, my Master sought flesh from the Savage people to the
south.

Gone a fortnight,
hee returned worse
then hee went forth.

(they set the woods afire in his flight)

4.

I would give foure-score and ten to be at home again
than see these Mountaynes of Ice aground
in sixescore fathome water.

5.

Then were the Master and the lame
driven from their Cabbins to the Shallop
while we broke Chests and rifled places.

                    nowhere near the *Iles of Goods merces*

It was bloud and revenge wee sought.

§

Sharking up and downe, one man asked
what to doe. I answered:
he should make an end
of what he starts
and strike while it is hot.

§

Their only friend, the Carpenter, got of them
a Peece, Powder, some Pikes, an Iron Pot,
and joined them on the dungeon Ice.

Then Greene cut the Shallop fast,
let our Main-sayle drop,
and toward the east we flew from them

as from an Enemy.

§

Was it me or someone else who asked

if ever wee reached home again,
why would wee not be shot?

6.

As from an Enemy,
we flew from them

(who we never saw again)

then were trapped in Ice
for fourteen daise.

After fourteen daise,
wee were readie to route
our Bosprite against the Rockes.

After fourteen daise, lustie men began to talke:

that the shippe should not come about any place
but keepe unto the Sea

that England was not safe for them

that we should find reliefe in naught but *Newfound Land*.

(I give God thankes we did not trie)

7.

Wee went ashore
in search of fowle and found naught
but broken ground and Rocke.

§

Then did John Thomas and William Wilson
have their bowels cut.

§

With his Knife, hee strooke me below my Pappe.

§

I sought for somewhat wherewith to strike him
and therewith strooke him
into the bodie and the throate.

§

Michael Perse and Henry Greene
came trumbling into the Boate.

§

As I rowed, Andrew Moter cryed
to bee taken in.

Greene cryeth *Coragio*!

and, with an Hatchet, I saw him ravage one
sprawling in the Sea.

§

Betooke them then
to their Arrowes
and their Bowes,
the Savages.

8.

So our Master had named this Land : *Desire Provokes.*

9.

I will saye it was with fear
to Ireland then wee stood

with winds for many dayes
and victuals for many less.

§

With naught to eat but Candle-grease,
some so weake they could not stand
and were saine to sit.

Juet dyed for meere want.   he fell into a fit

§

Unto the Bay of *Galloway*
where we pawned our Geere
for Beefe and Beere.

Then wee eight of twenty-three
the last men of the Discovery
came unto *Gravesend*
where for mutynie
was I taken.

like the ruins of ancient castles
after Alexander MacKenzie

We began our voyage with a course,
south by west, and a curse
against the weather. The Canadians
(primed and loaded) remarked to the air,
'It is a great evil to be exposed
on the banks of the Saskatchiwine river,
one white sheet of foaming water
the colour of asses' milk.

Upon a tree I engraved my name,
killed a buffalo and two grisly
and hideous bears and left them
where they fell, observed Jupiter's
first satellite and desired her –
clad in leather, handsome beaver
and rabbit-skin. My Darling project
come to me with no other canopy than the sky!

Then I dreamed myself once more
surrounded with my people.
They had a most wretched appearance:
low in stature,
their eyes small,
a swarthy yellow, lusty make,
the organs of generation uncovered.
But I secured their confidence with trinkets,
treated them with sugar
and hung halfpence
in the children's ears.

In fear, they lost the power of utterance
and displayed the most outrageous antics:

    Man
    Woman
    What?
    Stone
    Fire
    Tongue

'Do not you white men know every thing?'
Yes.
We possessed the power to starve them.

From the Frozen Ocean
across the snowy plains
even to the Hyperborean
on the earth in its virgin state,
here my voyage terminates.

Of that which we have a right to claim?
So much more remains.

The Voyages of Martin Frobisher
after George Best and Edward Dodding

1. [They] in search for a passage to Cathaia (1576)

We had bene vtterly lost
                    We thought these places might onely be called the Isie Seas
and we could not tell where we were
                    They shall get them into the latitude of ____ and ____
We sought to find the rich countrey of Cataya
                                        these poore men of Bristow
where all the sands and clifts did so glister
            faine to submit themselues to the mercy of the vnmerciful yce
yet we haue not found any
            and therewith like to be brused in peeces and perish in the sea
We weyed ancker
                    They saw themselues certaine people of that countrey
We wrote our letters
                                        Meta Incognita
We could perceiue
                    They found themselves without sight of Sunne
We sawe many monsterous fishes
                    They eat raw flesh and are of the colour of a ripe Oliue
and strange foules
                    They be more then by writing can be expressed
Into a ring we cast our selues vpon our knees

They haue not seene the thing whereof you aske them

and gaue God humble thanks

and by signes declared they wil stop their eares

We left toyes

and vnderstand you not

belles

They will teach vs the names

kniues

of each thing

pictures of men

in their language

and women

They beleeve we can make them liue

We all beleeued

or die at our pleasure

yet by no meines

They worship the deuill

can we apprehend

and they made signes vnto vs

any of them

that they had seene gold

2. [He]: upon the death of Kalicho (1577)

I was summoned
>> *quenching the fire*
> before imminent
>>> *inflammation*
>> death.
> *gaping*
When he was among us
>>> *the body neglected*
>> everyone's judgment
>>> *dissected*
>> was deceived.
> *putredinem*
>> There was
>>> *two ribs broken*
>>>> you might say
>>> *ulcer of the lung*
'Anglophobia'
>>>> *Anglium diceres metum*
>>> which he had
>> *dropsy*
>>> when he first arrived.
>>> *bloodletting*
When he came back to himself
>>>> *standing on the shore*
>>> from the deep
>>> *he sang clearly*
>> and summoned up
>>> *his last words*
in our language

                    the foolish, too uncivilized man
                              'God be with you.'
          Kalicho
He died.
     Calichough
                    Quite enough!
                              Callicho
     I was bitterly
          Calichoe
                              grieved
                    Calichoughe
          for our most gracious
     Cally Chough
Queen
               Callichog
                         how he
                    Collichang
     slipped through
          Caliban
                              her
     this Inuit man
                    fingers.
          Kalisuuq

3. [Drawing them out]: Frobisher's Captives

[Fight between Frobisher and Eskimos
watercolor (?) in Baffinland
(capture scene)
last seen   Munich in 1776
Metropolitan Museum of Art
(HB 24 415)
Kalicho   full-length in oils
with bow and arrows and paddle
Drawing in native dress
sealskin jacket with hood and tail
carried aboard the 1577 voyage
now in Zurich Zentralbibliothek 1964
standing to front and looking to right
Full-length   in oils
Fig. 8a.
Three busts [Full-length
kayak and ship in background
Rijksuniversiteit te Gent]
with names inscribed:
'Arnaq and Nutaaq'
(78 E 54; ff.410v.-410v.)
location now unknown
Portrait
last seen in 1688
in the British Museum (1989)
with bows and arrows
1577 Captives
caption: 'To send overseas
captured in oil
and English dress
for the Queen'

Imports into the Ports of London and Rochelle in 1743

153,830 Beaver

110,005 Racoon

45,055 Martins

16,832 Bears

13,058 Otters and Woodshocks, or Fifhers

10,280 Grey Foxes and Cats

3,117 Wolves

2,330 Cats, i.e. Lynx

1,710 Minx

692 Wolverenes

451 Red Foxes

440 Deer

130 Elks, i.e. Stags

120 Squirrels

Labrador

A land named for what was wanted from it:
fifty (some say fifty-three or that the Latin 'L'
was mistranslated to seven) Beothuk or Mi'kmaq (no
one knows which), their breath condensing/
disappearing/condensing like empty speech
scrolls in the autumn air. The ship (flickering
into and out of existence) slick with salt
and sick as the kidnapped (in the thinnest
of footnotes) are marched from the port
at Lagos (in books browned by age) – across
Avenida dos Descobrimentos, past Kebab Bollywood
and the Shaker Bar – to the Mercado de Escravos
where, on October 19, 1501 (the documents
confirm), they disappeared into labour.
A day like any other: the sun white
as a picked bone, memory busy erasing
itself in Portuguese, and the grey clouds
scudded over galleons (I would make this
pretty) heavy with rain and half-naked men
and women in chains.
The books by white men I have read
contain no record of the captives' display
in the streets where, soon, a bored king
would loose a rhino upon an elephant
for sport – it sniffed and turned away.
This is the contract history keeps.
Their bodies measured, sold, or thrown
down the Poço dos Negros (the Well
of the Blacks) where, 500 years later,
skeletons are found while digging a parking lot.
We read and cry our little bundles of shame
as the mind plods over and back over
and back these few spadefuls of text –
the sixteenth-century French of a Venetian ambassador,
the Italian of a spy –

'This is not
a great place.'

'the two-room museum
makes you experience
emotional pain'

'filled with smoke
and half naked men'

'They should abolish
this chilling little museum
and make it a new
cultural centre
for tolerance
and peave.'

'A slave market is NOTHING
to be proud of!'

'Not worth the €1.50.'

'A ripoff.'

38

                    'Of homini et de women

they kidnapped,
                et brought them to the King.

      I, Alberto Cantino,
            I, Pietro Pasqualigo,
               saw
                          touched
          et examined them.
              Like gipsies.
                  Arms, shoulders, and legs
        so well proportioned.
Faces marked with great means,
                       et them by signs
                como de them Indians.
Speech, it cannot be understood buy anyone
            but for that it is altogether human.
The dona has small breasts
          et belissimo body.
        The male
much more negro.
                They say the ship came
      2800 milia
    from a land of the north wind,
        a sea frozen over with snow.
        From this, the most Sérénissime King
hopes to profit greatly
        from wood for ships
and from the men
      who will be excellent for labour,
    the best slaves yet seen.'

becaufe that no man did euer fee this land before
after Thomas James

Out of the Ocean
wee feele another Sea

and our Ship labours
with another motion.

All this day, did beat,
were beaten

farefully amonst the Ice
in a tearing ftorme at north.

The Ship did fwag and wallow
as the winde fnuffled and ftormed.

No Cloathes were proofe againft it.
No motion could refift it.

Nofes cheeks and hands
froze white as paper.

Nights long I fpent
in torment

beneath more Starres in the firmament
then euer I had feene.

The Chirurgion took off the Gunners legge
at the gartering place.

We found the place where the Saluages had beene
but it was so long since.

Seuenteene poore foules
in a priddy Ship.

Wee haue not difcouered kingdoms
nor taken fpeciall notice

of their Magnificence
but vnder thefe heapes of ftone

men lye,
the famous marke of our Difcouery.

Linguisticers
after John Davis

: a boat
: go fetch

: come hither
: I meane no harm

: kisse me
: my sonne

: go to him
: give it to me

: no
: will you have this?

: music
: iron

: a knife
: a fog

: a tongue

La dicte terre
after Jacques Cartier

1. with such infection did this sickness spread

Ameda or Hanneda or annedda
or Arbre de Vie, wrote or said
or was reported to say – in English
handknotted through Italian
and French yet still carrying
the stench of gummes so rotten
all the flesh did fall off – Cartier,
mid–St. Lawrence, scorbutic,
his boat pestilent and fast-propped
against yce two fadomes thicke.

As Domagaia or Domagaya or
– 'Imagine that you are Dom Agaya.
What was is lik to leave your home
lands and live in France? What was
challenging? How did you feel?' –
the son of Donnacona showed them
(or the women did): boiled cedar
released ascorbate to make a drinke
the best ever found on this earth
(how near death I'd need to be
to write of bark tea like that?).
But in the rush to stop themselves
from dying here, it was so much better
than any prayer they hurled against it.

In 6 days, they stripped one tree bare.

When Rougemonte, Philippe, 22,
sank beneath the unknowen sickness,
the cappitaine ordered his body ripped.
Inside, they found a heart
bianco & putrefatto, lungs
blacke and mortified.
Gutless, they wrapped him
and buried his body overboard
between the snow and ice
that cracked its teeth day and night,
or so was wrote, against
the wooden hold.

2. language of the land newly discovered

: the sky
: la terre
: the sun

: the wind
: *il mare*
: the waves of the sea

: la neige
: some one is dead
: look at me

: where do you come from
: ilz appellent leur dieu
: where is he gone

: let us go to the boat
: give me a knife
: ung hachot

: a bow
: *mio fratello*
: that is worthless

: my sister
: sing
: laugh

: cry
: dance
: my friend

: run

Naming It
after James Cook

at the Masthead the Officer called out that he saw land which I named New Island because it is not laid down in any Chart and I hoisted an English jack and took possession in the name of His Britannick Majesty calling them by the same names as the natives do which was their idea of the sound of the name of Poverty Bay which I named because it afforded us no one thing we wanted so I named it Young Nicks head after the Boy who first saw it and _____ on account of its shape and figure and Cape Kidnapper for two or three paid for this daring attempt with their lives in Honour of which I have named it Hicks's bay because he was the first who discover'd it and we did not learn that the Natives had any name for this River of Man groves which after displaying the English Colours I took formal possession of in the Name of His Majesty and named the river Thames which occasioned my giving it the Name of Bream Bay in honour of Point Pocock (after this they began to Pelt us with Stones) so I called it Cape Turnagain because here we returned to Doubtless Bay which I am confident was never seen or Visited by any European before us so I named it in honour of the Union flag and drank his Majesty's health in a Bottle of wine (and gave the Empty to a native with which he was highly pleased) for which I have named them the Traps because they lay to catch unweary Strangers like the Ramhead this point going into Plymouth sound on which account I called it Cape Farewell for reasons which will be given in their proper place and be known on the Chart by the Name of Blind Bay or Cape St. George we having discovered it on that Saint's day and on account of the ˄New Plants collected ~~of this sort of fish found~~ in this place I gave it the Name of ~~Sting-Ray Harbour~~ Botany ist Bay when I caused the English Colours to be display'd and an inscription to be cut upon a Tree setting forth the Ship's Name, Date, etc. which occasioned my giving it the name of Point Danger above False Bay overlooking the Islands of Direction with Cape Upstart in the distance and Mount Warning which very much resembles Glass Houses which occasioned my giving them that Name besides these we saw some Bustards such as we have in England which occasioned my giving this place the Name of Bustard Bay and then Thirsty Sound by reason we could find no fresh Water so I named them Hope Islands because we were always in hope which I named after the Ship *Endeavour* and this island where the ceremony was performed I named it Possession

this country of science

my soul

Animal Electricity
after Luigi Galvani

Little flames, fixed fires
that certain men give out
when walking
or when silk garments are donned
in a very dark chamber.
Latent in the livid integuments,
it is a difficult thing to be known
even with electrophore
of dried nerve and bone.
Upon the caloric animalcules
dissected, I employed
an electrical machine
so that an eel, if bisected
transversely, trembled its tail
when a metallic arc was applied.
With current, a frog (hook secured
to its spine) jumped vigorously about,
while the wings of a chaffinch
slightly contracted.
Even stricken with a pinch
of pear powder or pernicious gases
(sometimes mephitic, sometimes opium,
powdered nicotine and arsenic),
a newborn cat moved its legs –
a phenomenon not lacking
with the head cut off.
Vipers have not yet been tested.
From the house high in the air,
we erected an iron wire,
hung upon it prepared frogs
and the legs of warm animals.
The thing went according to our desire.

Magnets
after William Gilbert

In the mingling exudations
of earths, metals, and juices,
in fitting matrices
from diverse precipitates,
lodestone perturbs the mind,
mostly kills.
Three scruples' weight
with sweetened water
restores young girls
when lacking colour.
Saffron of Mars.
Electuary of iron slag.
Brickle siderite.
Smeared with garlick
it does not allure.
From æquator to poles,
all interior parts conspire
to the greater love
of iron – its virtue bound
by an innate vigour.
Mingle in plaster
for fresh stab wounds.
Thus vainly and preposterously
do the sciolists look.
Let an experiment then be made
with fire.

Primum Frigidum
after Robert Boyle

1.

That Cold in its most frigorisick
exspiration be a thing
relative to our Feeling.
If the temper be chang'd,
the Object will appear more
or less to us. Its particles
vehemently agitate the Organs
of Touch. A cold superior.
With regard to the temperature
of the heavens, we do not easily
take notice of it. Air blows
out a pair of Bellows.
Matter is consider'd whilest in
a kind of Motion
through thermoscope
or vulgar weatherglass.
Only by unsuspected frigefactive Agents
are we disingag'd
from our grosser parts.

2.

In the morning:
pendulous in the water,
impellent in the slender pipe,
the tincted Liquor in the shank
as moist vapours abound
in the gelid Air.
How solid the Body is
yet how strong the adhesion
of its parts. Thought,
this Ambient Liquor, stretches
as one's spittle congeals
before it hits the ground.
Our Sensories, obnoxious
Blood, and analogous Juices,
open'd by the most subtile effluviums.
Confirmed by numerical Instruments,
spirits fly from the mingled Earth
we so commonly tread on.

Those Everlasting Orbs
after Galileo Galilei

Bringing my eye to the concave lens
like tongues, men present themselves
in the heavens emerging
from turbid mists where the dull
refuse of the universe has settled
down, uneven and sinuous.

Eminent men.
Famous men.
Men fixed and wandering,
magnified in size and fringed
with sparkling rays.

To have touched and put our lips
to these matters. To point out, as with
one's finger, the nature of those men
to whom we owe the erection
of permanent monuments,
ordinary and equestrian.

·   That the GALAXY is nothing but a mass of innumerable men in
    clusters – wherever you direct your telescope, an immense number of
    men immediately offer themselves to view.
·   When the men are observed with the naked eye, they do not show
    themselves according to their simple and, so to speak, naked size but
    crowned in uncurtailed glory.
·   And the milky lustre, like the whitish clouds of the Milky Way,
    dispersed through the ether? If you direct a glass to it, you will meet
    with a dense crowd of men, pulsating all around. The dance of them.
·   Some believe the light of the moon is but the reflected light of men or
    the rays of men penetrating her vast mass. This is so childish as to be
    unworthy of an answer.

- It is most beautiful and pleasing to the eye to look upon the man body, who, even if he be waxing, is by no means endowed with a smooth and polished surface but rough and uneven, crowded everywhere with vast prominences, deep chasms, and convolutions.
- Even certain planets have their periods around a certain man, now preceding, now following, never digressing.

I discovered these men, unshorn
in the midst of darkness.
Day by day I have seen them altered,
increased, diminished,
and destroyed.

They only derive from the shadows.

From a great orb
moving around the sun,
these are my observations.
I submit them to the judgment
and censure of right-thinking men.

Happy Countries, Happy Kingdoms
after Mercator

80°N, 220°E   The ocean here being absorbed
into the bowels of the Earth

80°N, 70°E   Here live Pygmies
also called Screlingers in Greenland

78°N, 130°E   Islands so far to the north
the Arctic pole appears southward

The Unfortunate Isles

72°N, 170°E   From sure calculations, here lies
the very perfect magnet
which draws to itself all others

64°N, 275°E   A sea of sweet waters
the Canadians say the limits are unknown

62°N, 112°E   Samogeds, that is: the people
who devour each other

59°N, 105°E   The Perosite, who with narrow mouths
live on the odour of roast flesh

38°N, 127°E   Here live men
who unearth the gold of ants

20°s, 270°E   Somewhere around here
some Indians
some large islands
gold abounds
Land of the Dwarfs

40°s, 305°E   Cannibals

           40°s, 295°E   In these parts, an animal
having under the belly a receptacle
in which it keeps its young

    45°s, 40°E   The Region of the Parrots

45°s, 315°E   Giant Patagonians

Here there be people who sail
with their backs
to our stars

Gold

For it is beaten and we are beaten for it:
crushed, mixed with mercury, stomped by foot.
Because of an uncharacterized glaciolacustrine unit
and an over-steepening of the downstream slope,
failure of the Mount Polley tailings pond
was attributed to the passive voice. The longhole up
plunge, down dip, and at depth. An unlikely event
officials repeated upstream from the town of Likely
and the T'exelc and Xatsull reserves. Rare.
He saw, then, some of the Indians wore gold rings
and choice blue stones in their nostrils and ears.
Auriferous. Lustful as any cyanide destruction circuit.
A nug, a lump, a rough unshapen mass. Like my father
before me, I too am a competent Nozzelman
needed for heavy lifting in the mucking cycle,
performing pre- and post-blast functions by hand
at, thank god, $23/h. Child to the sun.
After the Indians and mules were dead,
the English brought in slaves from Angola.
Rich as Potosi. The toxins were deadly
and certifiably organic. They held his feet
to flame until the marrow spurted and still,
for the life of him, he could not tell them
where they would find it.

For it finds its way to us and into us whether
through means magmatic, aeolian, or lithified.
The ore body attacked mercilessly
by percussive and rotary actions,
the hydraulic multi-boom jumbo hammering
the exposed rock face. *One covered my eyes,*
then they made me fall to the ground and tore off all my clothes.
Pulverized rock, cyanide, and water held in suspension
like doubt. Then they cut out her tongue. The loss
of containment was sudden: the quick-moving slurry
– trees, mud, debris, and waterborne arsenic –
raising the downstream lake. Fear retreated then
to the doré body and High Grade Zones.
Little thought to standard grind and carbon-in-pulp
extraction. Little care for how it glows golden
white on skin. One of the cleanest lakes in the world
now the country's most urgent news release.
Six nines fine. Buried deep in Manhattan granite.
It fell with such weight to the bottom of Lake Texcoco
held in the arms of men.

For it is malleable and fit to any purpose.
'Seekers of gold dig much, find little' or so said
Heraclitus, gold digger, speaking to the media
at the wildcat mine as the army torched the town.
'Dead metal,' Paracelsus added, 'vulgar,
without a soul.' Convulsions. The tailings pond
'near drinking-water quality' though the Do Not Use
advisory is indefinite. Blood in the urine.
After removing his Rolex, the disgraced geologist
jumped from the Alouette and plunged
into the Busang. Cast in the highest-quality alloys,
pyrochemical molten salts, and riverine tailings.
First the ears, then the nose and lips – and still,
though dying to tell them, she did not
know where they could find it. Chiselled
from permafrost, Frobisher's 'Black Ore'
good for nothing but metalling roads in Dartford.
Confusion. It holds a bite's indent
as cyanide leaches through the heap. Now
everything I touch, even the circuits
of this keyboard as I type: 'First they rackt him,
fastened his Neck to a post, two men holding
his Hands as they poured the molten gold
down his open throat.'

For we are fuel for its beneficiation
or its overburden. At the edges you can see
how Rembrandt applied gold leaf then buried it
beneath coat after coat of oil paint
through which now shines a golden sheen.
The underhand cut and fill. Pounded for days
between animal skins, then brushed on wet gesso:
one metric ton of Mexican gold to gild
the Catedral de Santa Maria de la Sede.
Burnished with dog teeth.
After the second tower fell, his first thought
was not pity for those who had died,
fear it would happen again or anger
at those who had done it, but 'buy gold.'
Tender. Barely legal. A safe haven
in this uncertain future. Hushing and booming,
they pried crowns from the dead for the Department
of Economy and Administration.
Brushed with gold dust, she raised her arms
high above the rising lake. Infinitely fungible.
The company remains committed
to rehabilitating the affected zones.
Since no human could need so much,
the Aztec assumed the horses ate it.

Notes

Early European narratives of exploration and contact with the 'New World' often intertwine the languages of scientific discovery and colonization and bring along with them all the attendant European concerns of race, commercial exploitation, and male domination over muted landscapes and the peoples who inhabited them. In writing and researching *Dead White Men*, I was interested in looking to these past stories (especially those focused on North America and the South Pacific), not to add to the fictions of past white heroism but to better understand the problematic relationship between the stories, the mythologies they have become, and the lands and peoples they describe. For many settlers, our understanding of the history of the land upon which we live is often limited to the names that have been given to it by past white explorers and the mythologies we have built up around exploration and discovery. I wanted to use poetry to interrogate this past and the texts upon which it rests.

This is the mandate of this book. This is the manner of its history.

Text for many of the poems has been collected from seminal exploration and scientific publications listed below. For many poems, transcription or translation errors have been maintained.

- 'All Well' excerpts from the journals of John Franklin's Arctic land expedition. The title is from one of the expedition's last notes, which was found beneath a cairn on Qikiqtaq.
- 'The Tragicall End of Henry Hudson' samples the journals of Abacuk Pricket, which detailed the fourth voyage of Henry Hudson in 1610, the crew's mutiny in what became Hudson Bay, and the return of the mutineers to England.
- 'Like the ruins of ancient castles' collects text from Alexander MacKenzie's *Voyages from Montreal through the Continent of North America to the Frozen and Pacific Oceans in 1789 and 1793*, Vol. II.
- 'The Voyages of Martin Frobisher' is built, in part, upon George Best's 1578 work on Frobisher's three voyages and contemporary descriptions of drawings made of the Inuit captives brought back to Europe as well as the many names given to Kalisuuq. I've also repurposed Edward Dodding's 1577 autopsy report which details the sickness and death

of Kalisuuq. Although the report could easily be seen as a quaint scientific document from its time, I think it important to remember that it is rooted in the death and descration of a real Inuit man; I hope the peom brings some semblance of respect back to his death.

- 'Labrador' recombines the translated letters of Alberto Cantino and Pietro Pasqualigo (which detailed their observations of the return of two ships, with their captives, from the voyage led by Gaspar Corte-Real across the north Atlantic in 1501) as well as Trip Advisor reviews of the Antigo Mercado de Escravos in Lagos, Portugal, which would have been the likely endpoint for the kidnapped slaves.

- 'becaufe that no man had euer fee this land before' excerpts samples from the *Strange and Dangerovs Voyage of Captaine Thomas James, in his intended Difcouery of the Northweft Paffage in the South Sea* (1633)

- 'Linguisticers' uses words from the vocabulary of thirty-nine Inuit words collected by John Davis on his second voyage in 1586 to Greenland and Baffin Island.

- 'La Dicte Terre' draws samples from the many translated versions of the journals of Jacques Cartier.

- 'Naming It' excerpts text from James Cook's journals from his first Pacific voyage to Tahiti and Australia.

- 'Animal Electricity' uses text from Elizabeth Licht's 1953 translation of Luigi Galvani's *De viribus electricitatis in motu musculari commentarius*, originally published in 1791.

- 'Magnets' samples Paul Fleury Mottelay's 1893 translation of William Gilbert's *De Magnete, Magneticisque Corporibus, et de Magno Magnete Tellure*, originally published in 1600.

- 'Primum Frigidum' uses specimens from Robert Boyle's *New experiments and observations touching cold, or, An experimental history of cold begun to which are added an examen of antiperistasis and an examen of Mr. Hobs's doctrine about cold*, originally published in 1665.

- 'Those Everlasting Orbs' rewrites Edward Carlos's 1880 translation of Galileo Galilei's *Sidereus Nuncius*, originally published in 1610.

- 'Happy Countries, Happy Kingdoms' excerpts text from the 1932 translation by the International Hydrographics Bureau of Gcrardus Mercator's Nova et Aucta Orbis Terrae Descriptio ad Usum

Navigantium Emendate Accommodata, originally published in 1569.
- 'Gold' incorporates text from a variety of sources from news articles on the Mount Polley mine disaster, to a report on human rights abuses at Barrick's Porgera Mine, mining job descriptions, and historic texts about the search for gold in the Americas.

The illustrations interspersed throughout are based on the following publicly displayed statues:
- Samuel de Champlain – sculpted by Hamilton McCarthy (the statue famously holds its astrolabe upside down), displayed in Ottawa, Nepean Point.
- Sir John Franklin – sculpted by Charles Bacon and displayed in Spilsby, England.
- John Cabot – sculpted by Guido Casini and displayed in Montreal's Cabot Square.
- Jacques Cartier – sculpted by Joseph-Arthur Vincent, the original is now in the Place-Saint-Henri Metro in Montreal.
- Joseph Banks – displayed in Sir Joseph Banks Park, Botany Bay, Sydney, Australia.
- George Vancouver – sculpted by Penelope Reeve and displayed in King's Lynn, England.
- James Cook – sculpted by Thomas Woolner and displayed in Sydney, Australia.

Interwoven with the full statues are close-ups of Kitchi Zibi Omàmìwininì Anishinàbe, a statue of an Indigenous scout created by Hamilton McCarthy in 1924 to kneel at the foot of his statue of Samuel de Champlain displayed at Nepean Point overlooking the Ottawa River in Ottawa, Canada. After complaints from the Assembly of First Nations about the statue's subservient position and demeaning clothing, it was relocated in 1999 to a nearby park where it currently resides, crouched in the bushes. The images of this statue are from a photograph by Jeff Thomas (and used with his permission) which were featured in his installation 'Why Do The Indians Always Have to Move?'

Acknowlegements

This book was written while living in Ottawa on unceded Algonquin territory and during a residency in Brisbane, Australia, on the traditional land of the Turrbul People.

Thanks to Coach House Books – especially my editor, Susan Holbrook, and Alana Wilcox – for all their support and editorial acumen. Thanks as well to other artists and writers who have helped along the way, however tangentially; special thanks to Chris Jennings and Brecken Hancock for long poetic discussions at the Manx. Unending gratitude to Katherine Battersby for her love and sustenance.

Poems from this book first appeared in the *Malahat Review,* the *Fiddlehead,* and Touch the Donkey. I would also like to acknowledge funding support from the Ontario Arts Council and Arts Queensland during the writing of portions of this book.

Typeset in Huronia, designed by Ross Mills between 2005 and 2011. Huronia is a massive type family that pushes the extents of the OpenType format by offering all Latin-based character sets, Greek, Cyrillic, Cree Syllabics, Cherokee, and the International Phonetic Alphabet.

Printed at the Coach House on bpNichol Lane in Toronto, Ontario, on Zephyr Antique Laid paper, which was manufactured, acid-free, in Saint-Jérôme, Quebec, from second-growth forests. This book was printed with vegetable-based ink on a 1973 Heidelberg KORD offset litho press. Its pages were folded on a Baumfolder, gathered by hand, bound on a Sulby Auto-Minabinda and trimmed on a Polar single-knife cutter.

Edited by Susan Holbrook
Illustrations by Shane Rhodes
Designed by Shane Rhodes and Alana Wilcox
Author photo by Pedro Isztin

Coach House Books
80 bpNichol Lane
Toronto ON M5S 3J4
Canada

416 979 2217
800 367 6360

mail@chbooks.com
www.chbooks.com

Note

While on a four-month residency in Brisbane, Australia, in 2013, I started a project of reading and poetic response that would last three years. This project focused on texts produced during the 1769 measurement of the transit of Venus. The transit – which was observed and recorded by over 170 observers at 77 posts around the world – was one of the most significant international scientific co-operations of its time. By measuring the movement of Venus across the Sun, accurate numbers could finally be calculated for the distance from the Earth to the Sun, the size of the solar system, and, more generally, our place in the heavens. The Royal Society of London for Improving Natural Knowledge sent out three main expeditions to measure the transit. Captain James Cook was sent in the *Endeavour* to Tahiti (which had only been recently discovered by Europe) with the additional orders to search for 'Terra Australus' – a conjectured land in the South Pacific. William Wales and Joseph Dymond were sent to Fort Prince of Wales in what is now Churchill, Manitoba, to complete the first European astronomical expedition to the Canadian Arctic. William Bayly and Jeremiah Dixon were sent to Honningsvåg and Hammerfest in Norway. As well, Christian VII of Denmark commissioned Maximilian Hell and his assistant, János Sajnovics, to travel to Vardø, Norway.

The texts from these voyages, though sometimes in different languages and set in such disparate places around the world, are unified in their focus on navigational and scientific observation as well as the exploration of the lands, peoples, cultures, flora, and fauna encountered. Taken together, they lay bare a one-sided view of seventeenth-century European thought – and the conjoined discourses of scientific exploration and colonization – at its very edges. Working with original and electronic copies (whether the electronic copy of Cook's journal kept by the State Library of New South Wales or William Wales' original handwritten astronomical observations preserved in an old envelope in the Thomas Fisher Rare Book Library in Toronto), transit uses the same strategies of discovery and exploration to attempt its own voyage through text.

Februarius.

...tus Satellitum ♃ apparens tubo astron. temp. Civili man...

.4		.3	○	.4 .2	
	.4	.1	○	2.	
		.4 2.	○	1.	.3
		.4 .1	○		3.
○			○	.2 4. .4	
		3. 2.	○	.1	.4
	3.	.2	○ .1		.4
		.3	○	.4.2	
.3.		.1	○	2.	
		2.	○	1.	.3 ... 4.
		.4	○		3.4
			○		
○			○		4.
○		2. .2	○		4.

...tus Sol illustrat... pro tuto...

| .4 | | | | | |

with wind Whifling all round the Compass nothing in sight but sea and sky as we search for home and some new occasion of sorrow (which Physicians have gone so far as to esteem a disease under the name of Nostalgia) last night a booby made us a visit and slept in our stomachs so we lay beating from fide to tide and stood to flurries a Sloop to Windward bound to Lisbon we lost Sight of them abreast Cape Farewell the Fleet to Windward in the Morning the breeze bound to Falmouth and contrary winds with which we were troubled all the way to Ireland then at Noon we saw land from the Mast Head which we judged to be Land's End and I here clofe my account of the ships means and ways with the Wind with which we ran

having breamed her bottom (so much eaten by the worm) we began to Shoalden and failed out of the river with a fine breeze from the weft set up the Topmast and Steeringsails but then did the west Wind die due to unfavorable breezes and the Sailmaker's Assistant died repairing the Wind and the Seamen now fell sick in the night and died Mr. Monkhouse at first light and I have got the Gripes I have got the Gripes I shall die I shall die as Yesterday amok Ditto Winds West and Gales Ditto Fevers and fluxes Ditto Daniel Preston and Forby Sutherland departed this Life and ditto Our hogs and fowls begin to die apace and here my airy dreams of entertaining my friends in England with the scenes that I am to see are vanishd and one more of the people died before I quit this part of the world I took down the infir'uments packed them up and put them on board the (hip where all hands were constantly employ'd repairing the dying Winds and with nothing in sight but sea and sky I pray the heart of this long-winded gale is broke

; They have all fine white Teeth they Climb like Munkeys Their natural Dispositio

lips Their progress in Arts or Shoes of {oft-tanned moofe hide they would steal bu

ll white except the Tip of their wings and Tails They are of a reddish Colou

anner of using them they were all naked except for their Privy parts They shoul

had stol'n from us They are Lazy and amuse themselves by singin

ns they inhabit They eat the bodys of their enemies they agreed to come and slee

k long and firaight they will not kill us but they have got no meat The Character c

bered with a fuperfluity of flefh They compute time by the Moon They felt th

ey observe the bright filament of the Sun They lay upon the Water and hol

gers they began to shake their Spears and Paddles at us They repel intruder

erfect account of the deluge where they fubftitute a beaver for the dove They felt hi

ft Aire they set up the War dance They lay in the Latitude of 28 degrees 8 minute

ran away as fast as they could They pointed to it and called it hom

refume my journal:

You are likewise to observe the Genius, Temper, Disposition and Number of the I

They have breeches made of feal fkin they are thieves to a man Short flat Noses an

everything that came their way they were far from afraid or surprised they paint their Bodies in St

nearly resembling that of rusty iron mixd with oil Especially their Mechanics Tools

not at first be alarmed with the report of Guns They are Ficus tinctor

They are the natural and in the strictest sense of the word the legal possessors of th

n my tent Their notions of Astronomy are principle objects of attention Their hair

heir persons They believe of a future state of rewards and punishments They seem

Smart of our Arms They are very fond of painting themselves with Red C

heir fins up in a very odd manner Dragging the Dead body they are apt to pilfer from

whom are come to disturb them in the quiet possession of their country They have a

hands and other parts of his body they should be first entertained near the shore w

South They threw their stones They were of the Mackrell kind They are numerous

and 1 {hall now

under favorable vocabularies
my geography became my history

hounded by circles   orbs
neither identical or different

doubt became perception   a fast-moving cloudlet
more accurately monitored than described

black particles fell
from the edge of the sky

Are you a description of the Transit of Venus?

we were blown to a Harbour where we could repair our defects which we discover'd most grave and people as tall as Europeans very dark brown but not black not belonging to the King certainly not unentertaining not made of {alt water nor had they woolly frizled hair nor had they any weapons but their faces and bodies painted with ^{a sort of white paint or Pigment} so we gave them a peppering of small Shott (the clothes we had given them – all in a heap) and got down the Topgallant yards the Foretopgallant mast the Jibb Boom the Spritsailyard unbent the Mainsail and seeing a man fall (a few drops of blood) we continued until noon and saw 6 or 7 more and we examin'd all their Noses and I do not know why I may not keep one as my neighbours do lions and tygers

a Gentle williwaw

in the falling little wind

so small that at any other Time

but now

a trolly lolly

the Wind

the least puff

the Sea

the voice of God

within the breaking surf

a Small Air

a breeze

the sweetest of Zephyrs

nothing

blows Fresh, blows strong

a gust

which died away

a Shoal

the Ship Struck and stuck fast and began to make water as much as two Pumps could free (the Ocean once our Assylum we now look'd upon with terror) which muft be the inevitable deftruétion and the total demolition of our aerial fabric but then there blows directly upon us at this Critical juncture

More Translations of the Lappish Language

Their Words for Sounds

: a gently running stream whirring over river rocks

: an animal in the water splash

: wolves singing when I cry ass drunk

: a fire salt sprayed

: a bow when the arrows are shot out

: knocking as I roll down the hegyrs

: an empty vessel when tapped by two empty containers

: water falling in a fire

: a tree mouse gnawing Girr

: sand between your teeth or a ball stuck in a tube

: knocking a fish

: a dog that flatters

: noisily sipping like when someone eagerly drinks

: sometimes here this sound when the larynx nip slips

we no sooner landed than we saw the Lappish character the vices virtues and various customs of the Lapps and Lappish dances and I made enquiry as to the exiftence of the aquatic animals called Karaakens whofe dimenfions appear to me to be far beyond the fcale of nature and we shall find it that what makes the Wind raise a considerable sea in the Seamen – such people as can be spared to the weather or dashed to pieces in a Moment or lashed for not doing duty or given to scamped work or committed to rash action or exercised at small arms or employ'd overhauling the rigging or making rope or given to the detestable Vice of Sodomy or washed overboard and left to the Breezes – we employ'd Caulking the Winds without the least Variation so while the Ship lay fast and the wind freshen'd we got out before her which obliged us to bear away with land seen by the Flashes of lightening wherein was heard the sound of surf upon the reef which might prove the ruin of both ourselves and all the sails which made our weathering the gulf of Wind and the depth of water unfathomable and we saw the breakers again within us so I called it ˌCape Tribulation because here begun all our troubles

I saw a very extraordinary curiosity

it hops

and how embarrassing it will be to these meticulous observers of the magnetic needle when they learn of my unquestionable theory and read my extremely accurate observations and I had reason to think then it was in my power to look into the Variables of the winds then a Water Spout in the North-West about the breadth of a Rainbow but this was a very favourable wind indeed so shipping against Southerly Winds and having but Hazey weather which blows against our crazy ship being very Leakey in our upper works with the Capstan and Windlass and the cumbrous hempen We judged it to be a Kangooroo (its nature, disposition, and character minutely noticed) a leaping quadruped or _{^a} ^{Kanguru} with the Track of a Dog as black as the Devil with 2 horns on its head (I dard not touch them) but very good eating and abominably saucy I espied among the common croud a very pretty girl with a fire in her eyes and saw (what is a sin in Europe is simple gratification in America) the truest picture of an arcadia of which we were going to be kings

Nails were temptations they could not withstand so a spike for a small pig a smaller for a fowl a hatchet for a hog and we kept beating to windward with all the sail we could Crowd and fmall goofeberry bullies fome flrawberries many cranberries and (these victims of Astronomy) 12 lashes each for refusing their allowance of Fresh Beef but we were sure of meeting with nothing but Wind which blew like vowels in the congested airspace so to speak they are CANNIBALS (we $_\wedge$^{therefore} resolved for the future not to despise Dogs flesh) and following the dog watch William Greenslade Marine either by Accident or design went overboard and was Drowned and what winds we had were against us but then a breeze sprung up at South and imerg'd behind the moon's dark limb (very exact) not permitting us to look into the winds they could not keep so we set the Topsails double close upon a fresh Gale of the solar wind but (taken between flying clouds) feveral of the above Obfervations are a little un=certain and I have found the clock gaining 1'18" per day and the watch in total darknefs we Stood to a high rowling Sea and compared our reckonings for I have found these peoople may be frightned into any thing

the sky is the landscape occupied by the Sun
we plunged into the sun

How was I going to see
what was not there?

Then, to the naked eye, Venus stepped
in front of the Sun
and I fell forward over time.

Once you touch the inside –
O solar charger! O Helios! O solar wind!
Give me love, put it under
this harem of cloud.

Data is destiny. The more it seemed
to approach my heart,

the more it took place
at the bottom of a lens.

**This country of
science my soul**

Port
Desire,
Fort
Venus

_{in purfound silence} I hear nothing but murmurings Their treachery (which is unsurpassed and a result of their savage ideas) THEIR land THEIR wild animals and THEIR rights generally a Foul wind and little of it but soon a Wind coming to the North enabled us to go close to the Westward and a last gale from that Quarter with land in sight (it provd to be a cloud) makes one think there is no wind Coming so we stood close without seeing stood fast without being stood in without any difagreeable fenfations stood the whole night without any wind at all as the wind seem'd to incline on Shore so we stood off and gave it Shelter and made the best of our way making sail when the wind veer'd and making wind when serv'd turtle and greens so then we Tack'd with a prodigious swell rowling in and I saw or at least I thought I saw 3 hansome girls in a canoe (then heaven wholly covered over) but then she (her eyes full of meaning) displayd her naked beauties (letting drop a cloth that covered her) and ~~the Sun~~ broke through the clouds so I took her by the hand (with very little perswasion) and led her to the tents (my flame) and put her politeness to every test (it raised its grammar and I saw in it a wide array of rules) and penetrated farther into thofe bays and inlets the Openings and Passages and culmination sun shimmering dashed against the Rocks

(Venus stepped in front of the solar disk and showed me her parts)

I became suspicious that the iron oven
had affected our observations

Te Deum laudamus Father Hell observed this moment and a great sense of satisfaction spread among all the inhabitants of Vardø when the Sun came out from under a cloud with Venus upon it the bright crescent or rim of light encapsled all that part of her circumference with light Airs and Calm and the Wind already half spent as yesterday (the horizon of mist made the wind of Venus vibrate) we then amused ourselves in the collecting of gentle breezes but that proved very unsteady so when the ventus died we gathered a fresh gale to the Eastward and we saw something upon the furface of the fea – a Seal aSleep a Sea Lyon a stupendous worm (he judged the animal could not be lefs than twenty-five fathoms long) and some very small and ugly People – so we hauled to the Eastward though the wind continued at North-East and saw several of the Inhabitants (they had with them a Jackass – a sure sign Europeans had been among them) of a middle size very spare and thin of a copper colour so we veer'd round from South by East to North-North-East where the wind blowed a fresh Gale (which illuminated them native adorned and enhanced) then was gone and succeeded by hundreds of miles of raging wild winter and we could see clearly that their eyes were black and the mofl beautiful that I ever (aw so we set Topsails with one Reef out and stood to Westward where the Wind proved very unsettled for this day the captain's clerk had his ears cut off

a reward of fifteen guineas
to any one who should discover
the person or persons
who cut off the Clerk's ears

as the day of Observation now approaches a tent was set up but then overturned by a pig and I did not care to spend the little wind I had so we cast off the Hawser hove short on the bower carried out the Kedge blackened the yards and bent the sails to warp the Ship where we shelterd from all winds except those Winds that blow and several of the Natives came off to us in their Canoes more to look at us than any thing and to them we shewd the planet (Venus in limbo in two parts of the world) upon the sun and made them understand we came to see it and hauled off upon the weathermost wind and though we kept plying to windward all day and Kept plying to windward all night under close Reeft Topsails we examined the clock and found the pendulum to vibrate on each fide of nothing then an Atmosphere or Dusky shade round the planet with -42 at thermometer B the little alarm clock would not go so we made sail and steer'd North from the Winds that blew the exterior contact at the ingreff and we catch sight of the Sun's shiny filament when a light breeze sprung up the firy matter ˄^Lightning and the wind now quite against us we Reef'd the Topsails beating windward and though I thought the Winds of Yesterday would blow they appeard to us – the word contact is very doubtful – through our glasses and we fancied we could see (every one of them stark naked) their Colour when we could scarce distinguish whether or not they were men

a magnetized needle has not
the time or mind to think of verse

Translations of the Lappish Language

: he breaks the snow

: it falls to the snow surprise

: the fresh snow is not too deep

: the deep, broad features of snow (which no one has ever seen)

: person with frozen snow name

: they say this if the wind piles up the snow

: the children snowball effect

: I roll down the snow

: upon melting, snow remaining on the mountains

: the slushy, melting snow

: the wet snow that sticks to Lapp carts during migration

with a Cable on the Best Bower and a Hawser and a half on the Stream
we heaved down and were obliged to Tack when the wind not abating
nor subsiding bore away so in short all hands get abominably drunk
and we saw several Pintado Birds and some Turtle upon the Water and
splendid rays stretching themselves out long and numerous as luminous
particles speedily drifted from the cloud that's pretty with a great number
of small Whales about the {hip along with the grey-goofe the way-way
the brant the dunter very troublesome infects the mofchetto and the
{and-file so we hauld the wind to the South-West (which the wind would
not do) and close reefd the Topsails and notwithstanding a fair wind and
fine weather (they had got each of them a Wife and would not return)
and Doves about and Reefs without with hail and Airs I saw myself
this morning a little way from the ship and went to the main-top-mast-
head to be satisfied of the truth and there I saw the Wind Breathing and
moving so there I stood waiting for it open to the heard hearted winds

Lastly, Gentlemen, form a Vocabulary of the names given by the Natives to the several things and places which come under your Inspection.

Translations of the Tahitian Language

: row to me
: speak to me

: to pull one by the hair
: to squeeze, or press one

: a day
: a night

: an echo
: a fart

: to jostle, or shake
: to cram, or thrust into

: a smell
: a hole

: a song

my desire?

to be accurately understood in the sun

we deviated from weather with heavy rain only with rain with heavy
weather and showers of rain or squally with rain or Lightening and rain
or hazy with rain or attended with rain or very much rain all day or Hail
and Rain or Snow and Rain or rain and Snow or the night being dark
and rainy or the Day being light and drizzly or it rained very faft or it
rained very slow almoft all the time it rained to a very great Strain or a
constant refrain or (The sea is certainly an excellent school for patience)
Winds round their Heads with rain enough to knock Men's brains out
(is it any wonder if I lost my mood) as the grafs began to fpring up very
{aft in the bare places and the goofeberry bufhes to put out buds a wind
weltcrly ~~blowed~~ ^{blew} Very Strong (wind power all the nub) and I told 32
iflands of ice while two black servants perished in the night with cold and
the South-Westerly swells I have been speaking of constantly secured
us from all the winds we had not before discovered so we Kept plying
to Windward all night Plying to windward all this day and Plying to
windward all this afternoon without getting in the South-West Quarter
(for its not Southing but Westing thats wanting) and we made the ifland
of Refolution at the entrance of Hudfon's Straits and there came along
side of us three Eskimaux in their canoes while we waited for a Gentle
breeze to blow from Upper favage Illand to Utopia and Cape Fly Away

Nothing special today unless the great coldness of the wind from North is worth mentioning unless the entire air swimming with watery exhalations is news unless a dense fog exceeding thick is of interest unless dark Squals and Lightning are most curious things unknown in Europe unknown to me and these people unknown and dangerous but what Winds we have had this day set down in the journal beneath a close-reefed Maintopsail which caused us to Tack several Times and paff within a cable's length of a very large ifland of ice (it appeared to be nothing elfe) we Serv'd Slops to the Men put on our winter rigging saw the footsteps of people fresh upon the sand which Painted the Boat with a Genteel breeze and the fog {o thick we could fcarce fee a man on the forecafile then a fresh Trade wind with heavy Albetrosses all wings and Tails so we hauled our courfes when there came along a boat with feveral Elkim'aux women and we traded wind with the people (I saw what I took and left them in Strings of beeds)

with hard Storms of Rain I was enflamed by Wind and an unrestrained desire to reach those unexplored islands when I saw a dolphin and admired the infinite beauty of Wind South-East to South-South-East but he would not give us a chance of taking him Cloud Thunder Lightning Rain and Humming birds I also saw so we tended to the Wind and Hove it up with a Breeze and made Sail with the Caulkers Caulking the Sailors Sailing the Riggers Rigging and the Slaves well while I ohferved the {un's meridian altitude the cat killd our bird and a large swell of Gentle breezes blew northerly and I deduced a Suit of Sails a Storm of Rain and Leagues from Land Diomedea exulans Procellaria velox pallipes Latirostris longipes and Nectris fuliginosa (all put in spirits with heavy squalls) which brought us under our courses so we hauld this dirty weather loosed the Reef from the Foresail and wound up the Clock for we will remain a good long time at Sea

f like the Land of Brazil bearing West and Terra del Fuego falling in

ng Leagues and covered with Wood and Sand Land as it appeared

West by West the Land of the Sugar Loaf being so very high we were

nd mark should prove to be an **Island** discovered because we saw

eventing me from satisfying my Curiosity so we left the

nd land laying down again disturbed we faw other [hips under the

d of any extent very far from firm land we saw to the Westward

ch points of **land very hilly, very broken** so how should

er of ice iflands and the Great Surf which beat everywhere

having landed we could see nothing barren as this land

one intire forest and Our errand was to fee if we could not

North and something of this land was mentioned but knowledge

land is our land and this land was tolerable good but we

ve tack'd and had 57 fathoms with sand still Leagues from land

so we made this land I have Named and laid down upon paper

a piece of crumpled paper not wholy barren nor distinguished

S he was Eat by Man! Land we saw bearing South-East by East

liscover'd it who lived on it their customs their beliefs and we

icher for it for instead of sand I found land locked and on the

lis Majesty and the Natives assembled did not understand it

s and the land is not to be seen unless you are pretty high on this

this land and New Zealand we discover'd the land was no more

as the land it is the land it will be right where we were standing

I have laid down no land nor figured any Shore but what I saw
Land to the South-West Quarter Land which we judged in sight E
from the Ship a strand Hazey upon No Land in sight bearing N
forced to land there being nothing to hinder the command unless
land that we could not see took land we could not take and the land
land and we were not likely to fall in with again this most remarka
land discovered for England we left the Land for there is
land and found its whereabouts we saw to the Eastward th
our people land so far from Land on account of the great
and everything upon this land we discover'd in the mor
appears discover'd in the afternoon we saw from the Mast
find fome land likely to produce corn he pointed with his hand t
of terra incognita is only traditionary this land is an Islar
thought we saw imaginary land upon the body of land standir
and we saw it again more Distincter than at any time we had b
I raised the flag and dignified this land by calling it unev
by anything remarkable not rich not profitable no
so I demanded we quit this land altogether the nearness of it
shortned Sail in upon the Miles of lost ground but the land al
other hand we saw upon it people which I claimed in the nam
must be all Land and Water and reefs and forests and grasses an
craggy Land which soon died away and was Succeeded by the Sea be
THEIR land according to the Charts we made this Land the lan

Light
is now declared to be
of the highest importance
to the Royal Society

In 1767 I thought of nothing less than Venus
in this theater of Arctic Astronomy
and atmospheric brutality

everything included light
I should explain more clearly
clearly and openly

What ever do you have to think
outside of the Sun?

so another ship with the highly famous English astronomers Dymond and Wales set sail for Hudson Bay and the HMS Emerald to Honningsvåg and the Royal-Caesarian Astronomer Hell Míksa on 'The Duck' to the Polum Arcticum and the unspeakable wrath of the Artic Ocean and they kept no journals except for the moft part nafty thick and cold and wound up Clocks with heavy squalls Struck Topmasts and Top Gallant Yards and set up two astronomical pendulums one from Vienna and the other by the famous master Le Roy to compute the dimensions of the whole folar fyftem with 20 Pounds of Onion per man 3032 Gallons Wine 4 Pipes of Rum and lots of Wind for all West by South with some Rain and Squals within the lower Obfervatory we hung the Thermometer mark'd A and that mark'd B was hung without (Quicksilver in the Basin) two reflecting telescopes searching for a lost star I Found Yesterday doubtful before the mercy of the Wind

having settled my affairs in London West-South-West I went on board the bark ENDEAVOUR then lying in Galleons Reach Calm Clear and correct at 3 O'Clock in the even this one ship dispatched with a mission in the river Thames to take a correct observation of the Transit of Venus (glorious and honourable) on the 3rd of June 1769 (the Phenomenon) to determine (with certainty) the fun's parallax and to search for some extremely remote perfectly prepard even undifcovered winds of the Pacific (in Mind at least) weigd anchor with flying rain and the little dog Apropos too

then Fresh Gales with Rain

West and Gentle

Breeze with Light Airs

howls that heave

and lafhes moaning a murmur

mutters and nips a puff pants then arage roars and rufhes rips

nd fqualling scuds and shears

flanting and shrieking fnorts and snarls ftorming and

then soughs a sigh that shifts to fnuffles as fobs

twist and wail as wheezes whirl and whiff

then whiffles a whiffet then whiftles a whine

that whifks and wafts and winds

a whifper a whiffle a

airs

aloft a breath

breezes a **billow** blows

blasts a burst that blufters

backs and calms as currents draft

adrift **farts and flows** fluffs flutter

then freshen with fury as flurries groan and grow

to growls and gusts agafp galing and galling ar

and **huff to luffs** laughir

and ruffles fcreeching

stirring

whose souls shout out before the hungry sea
and nuclear test plutonium fallout,
                 give way to the wind that blows forever,
     and Natives (their Skins the Colour of Wood soot,
                              eyes black as jet) give way to Tahitians,
          Efkimaux to Inuit, Lapp to Sami,

          and a three-year journey gives way to the VenusTransit app,
with GPS and atomic clock, as Venus (caught
               in her heavens by a two-foot Gregorian
     reflector) spins at 1.7 metres
                              / second across the flat disk of the Sun
               which gives way to no thing and no one.

122

to God's wrath) may burn the observatory,
and though Cook's ship (in this Arcadia of which
we are now kings) may sink to lust and venery
as near 100 men pull every fucking iron nail
to trade for sex with the Tahitian women,
this is how darkness interstellar gives way

to compass and to calliper as the hull
of the flat-bottomed *Endeavour* gives way
to the calcareous plates of teredo navalis
(fat and full in the trellis of wood
it devours) and to the reef's calcium
carbonate towers, the people of Bola Bola

give way to the people of Ulhietea,
the mechanical clock to the cold's fiery torment,
the 'nameless' point to Cape Kidnappers (better,
by degree, than the Bay of Murderers),
the mucous membrane to the burning clap
(une maladie qu'on y attrape) and seamen,

and ship-butchering shambles, reflected (Venus

at Her Mirror) in polished copper and tin

(pit mined at Exmoor, polished in London)

strained through smoke-darkened glass and projected

to the retina, upside down and reversed, of a man

who notes with meticulous hand in the margins

of his book: that nothing might disturb

the Observation, no Indian was allow'd near us.

This is the blackdrop effect and the seventeenth century

of a way, as Halley said, to estimate

the vast distance of the Sun: Maximilian Hell

on a mud-covered hill in Vardø, his servant

shouting every second in Latin; Wales and Dymond

eighteen months in Churchill (a glafs of brandy froze folid

in the obfervatory) for a page of calculations.

Though the morals and equipment may be suspect,

though the co-operating nations may now be at war,

though the townsfolk (still wanting some mystery

Obferving the 1769 Tranfit of Venus

Not the Great Whore. Not Ishtar. Not some fading god
of rain and war. Not Saartjie Baartman (transported live
to Piccadilly, exhibited dead at the Musée
de l'Homme), not Venus Caelestis, cytherean,
bull-blood bright and most luminous in the night.
Not even Venus of the Pretty Bottom

(the hoped-for spectacle unoccluded
by untimely gloom) rolling retrograde
at 126,000 km/hour on the edge
of the Sun. And definitely not Venus Cloacina
at the moment of ingress (0:56:70),
purifier of the sewers and goddess of Local 503.

This is the Venus of White Men in Shorts
gazing down telescopes as if through a speculum
as two spheres (Venus and the Sun in the Wind
do shake) collide though 108 million km apart.
Venus (she hides behind thick Clowd) risen
from sea foam over terra incognita, its hidden shoals

transit

DEAD WHITE MEN

SHANE

RHODES